M000248142

Retire Wild, Free, and Happy

Do It Now with the Money You Have

By Jerry Minchey

www.LifeRV.com

Stony River Media

First edition copyright © 2018 v1 Jerry Minchey

All rights reserved, including the right to reproduce this book or portions thereof, in any form. No part of this book may be reproduced in any form without the express written permission of the author.

Minchey, Jerry. Frugal RVing / Jerry Minchey 2018.01

ISBN-13: 978-1-947020-08-5

1. Retirement living.

Published by Stony River Media

Knoxville, TN

StonyRiverMedia.com

Disclaimer

The information in this book is based on the author's knowledge, experience, and opinions. The methods described in this book are not intended to be a definitive set of instructions. You may discover other methods and materials to accomplish the same result. Your results may differ.

There are no representations or warranties, express or implied, about the completeness, accuracy or reliability of the information, products, services or related materials contained in this book. The information is provided "as is," to be used at your own risk.

This book is not intended to give legal or financial advice and is sold with the understanding that the author is not engaged in rendering legal, accounting, or other professional services or advice. If legal or financial advice or other expert assistance is required, the services of a competent professional should be sought to ensure you fully understand your obligations and risks.

This book includes information regarding the products and services of third parties. I do not assume responsibility for any third-party materials or opinions. Use of mentioned third-party materials does not guarantee your results will mirror those mentioned in the book.

All trademarks appearing in this book are the property of their respective owners.

Copyright © 2018 Jerry Minchey. All rights reserved, including the right to reproduce this book, or portions thereof, in any form. No part of this text may be reproduced in any form without the express written permission of the author.

Version 2018.01

Dedicated to my parents, Charles and Helen Minchey, who taught me to enjoy retirement living.

Table of Contents

Introduction

"You only live once, but if you do it right, once is enough."

~ Mae West

When I say to retire "wild," I don't mean you should start experimenting with drugs, go rob a bank or join a nudist colony. But I am talking about living a fun, more adventurous life where you don't worry as much about what other people think.

Conventional wisdom about retirement says to talk to a financial advisor and find out how much money you'll need for retirement. He will tell you how many millions you will need to retire and maintain your current lifestyle.

That's probably good advice if you're in your 20s, 30s, or 40s, but if you're nearing retirement age, you should face the fact that the money you have is what you have. There is not much you can do to change that number.

Even trying to change your investment strategies when you're nearing retirement age and trying to get 20% or 30% return so that you can reach some magical number of dollars for retirement could be disastrous.

1

You might be thinking that you're nearing retirement age and don't have nearly as much money as your financial advisor says you'll need. Do you keep working? What should you do?

There's a solution to how to retire when you don't have much money

The good news is you can retire with very little money and have a much better life than the high-priced retirement life your conventional-thinking financial advisor was planning for you.

This book is not about theory, philosophy or conventional wisdom. In this book, I'll show you how to make your retirement truly wild, free, and happy regardless of how much money you have.

Having a lot of money could be a detriment instead of the solution to a happy retirement.

The key is that you don't want to continue to live the high-priced lifestyle you're living now.

You want to live a different lifestyle when you retire

I'm sure you don't want to change everything in your life. You probably want to keep your dog (and maybe your spouse), but you would like to change about everything else.

You want to be wild, free, and happy when you retire.

Are you living wild, free, and happy now? I didn't think so.

My guess is that you're not experiencing any wild, free or happy things now. You're not doing anything that you would consider wild, different or fun. You're not living free by any means. You're not free to do what you want to do, go where you want to go, and you're not even free to make decisions about what you want to do.

If you're not living wild and free, then you can't expect to be happy. In other words, you're not experiencing any of these things. Your life is not wild, free or happy!

You can live this lifestyle without the millions of dollars financial advisors tell you that you need. You can do it on a dime and a dream. In the next chapter, I'll talk about the most important thing you will need to live this happy lifestyle. What you need is a dream. Then I'll talk about how to do it on a dime and in later chapters I'll even tell you how to get the dime you will need.

But first, living below your means most of the time will give you more freedom and a lot more joy.

Don't wait for things to get easier, simpler or better. Life will always be complicated. Learn to be happy right now. Otherwise, you'll run out of time. You will never have all the answers. Most of the retirees I talk to say their only regret is that they didn't do it sooner.

There are many reasons why people want to live a different lifestyle when they retire (of course, many people choose just to continue living the same boring lifestyle they have been living for years and then wonder why they're not enjoying their retirement).

Here are some of the reasons people choose to live a different lifestyle when they retire:

- Freedom

- Adventure

- Fun

- Inexpensive

- Relaxed lifestyle

- Exciting

- They want to do something different

The easy path is to do nothing and continue living basically the same lifestyle you're living now and in the same place. That's what most people end up doing. Yes, they make a few changes, but they don't come close to making enough changes to enjoy a wild, free, and happy lifestyle. Worse than that, they end up spending a lot of money living a life they don't really enjoy. What could be worse than that?

In a nutshell, if you're nearing retirement age, it's too late to try to decide how much money you will need for retirement. At this point, you need to look at the situation from the opposite end.

You have to look at the money you have and the income you'll have, and then decide what kind of retirement lifestyle you can enjoy with the money you have.

Face the facts. It is what it is at this point.

The good news is that if you follow the advice and information that have I provided in this book, I think you can live a retirement lifestyle that is way better and more fun than anything you have imagined and for sure more enjoyable than what your financial advisor was trying to get you to save and pay for.

I'm not a big fan of most of the things Mae West said, but I think she nailed it when she made the following statement I quoted at the beginning of the chapter.

"You only live once, but if you do it right, once is enough."

~ Mae West

Let's get started and find out how you can enjoy your retirement beyond anything you have ever imagined and how to do it on the money and income you have. You may be able to do it and not even touch your savings.

Bottom line: If you dream of living a life that you don't need a vacation from, keep reading and I'll show you how to do it, and, yes, I'll show you how to do it on a dime and a dream. Continue reading, and you will discover that it's your decision which lifestyle you live—your present lifestyle or one of the wild, free, and happy lifestyle I'll describe in this book.

You'll find that it's not a matter of whether you can afford to live a happy retirement lifestyle; it's a matter of do you want to? That is, do you want to enough to make some changes in your thinking?

Chapter 1

You Have to Have a Dream

"Go confidently in the direction of your dreams. Live the life you've imagined."

~ Henry David Thoreau

Do you have a dream of how you want to live when you retire and what you want to do?

By having a dream, I don't mean a dream such as, "I want to retire and not have to go to work" kind of dream. And I'm not talking about a daydream kind of dream.

I'm talking about what some people would call an unreal, crazy kind of dream—a dream that breathes new life into the dull routine of your day.

Imagine what it would be like to live anywhere you want to and be able to travel when and where you want to.

Hold that picture and thought in your mind and then compare that to the way your life would be if you retired and continued to live in the same place, doing the same thing every day that you're doing now.

Which way would you be happier? You can't decide until you start dreaming and picturing yourself living your ideal retirement lifestyle.

Nothing will happen until you start dreaming

When we were kids, we were always dreaming and playing make-believe. As we got older, dreaming was frowned on. Daydreaming was then considered to be goofing off.

Forget about the stigma that sometimes goes with dreaming and start dreaming right now for real.

And if your dreams don't scare you, maybe they're not big enough.

A lot of people think of a dream as wishful thinking. For example, they dream of winning the lottery.

But that kind of dream won't cut it. If you're going to make your retirement dream a reality, your dream must be more than wishful thinking. It must be a burning desire. It must be something you're going to make happen come hell or high water, as the saying goes.

You can afford to retire in style

Before we start talking about retirement dreams, I want you to get the thought out of your mind that you can't afford any of these things. You absolutely can, and, in later chapters, I'll be showing you how you can afford any of these lifestyles and not even dip into your savings.

You may be thinking that's impossible but trust me; by the time you finish reading this book, you will be convinced that it's not only possible, but the most important thing is that you can make it happen in your world—but first, you must start dreaming.

Here are some ideas to help you start dreaming

First, let me say that more than likely, none of the pictures and ideas I'll be describing below are what you dream of when you think about your retirement. I'm showing you these to get you thinking outside the box.

Don't think of these ideas as a place to move to and live from now on. No, think of these ideas and places as somewhere you might want to live and do for two or three months (maybe even for a year).

Also, consider these ideas as something you might want to do one time and never again, and also consider them as something you might like to do for a few months every year—at least for a while.

There's no one perfect place to live and retire. You've probably lived in the same place for years, and you know that it's too cold part of the time and too hot part of the time.

Also, there's nothing to do where you live now—at least nothing new to do. You've already done everything.

If you're not going to change anything in your life, why retire?

Eight retirement ideas to help you start dreaming

Probably none of the following eight retirement ideas are anything you would want to do when you retire. I'm not trying to change your mind or talk you into any of these adventures.

The whole purpose of describing these retirement lifestyles is to get you to start dreaming.

When you're considering ideas for what you want to do and where you want to live when you retire, keep in mind the fact that you don't (and probably shouldn't) plan on living in the same place all the time. I will go into the concept of living in more than one place when you retire in Chapter 10.

When you consider the following eight retirement ideas, ask yourself, *Would I enjoy living there for a month (or three months or six months)? Would I like to live there for a few months every year for a while or is it something I think I would like to do just once?*

Of course, it's also likely that when you consider each one of these ideas, you might think, "No way. I would never enjoy living there or doing that."

Deciding what you want to do when you retire is a lot easier when you think about what you would like to do and how you would like to live for periods of one, three or six-month increments. It's a much harder decision to buy a house and live somewhere forever more.

Later, I'll talk about how it's possible to live in different places and how to do it for much less than you're spending to live in one place now. But, for the time being, accept the fact that it's possible, and let your imagination go wild and start dreaming.

Here are eight off-the-wall retirement ideas to help you start dreaming

#1. Would you like to live in a castle for a few months?

There are plenty of castles around the world that you can rent for a few months at a time. You probably don't want to rent the whole castle—just a small section of it. I have a friend in Scotland who owns a castle, and he rents out sections of it. You probably don't want to live this lifestyle permanently, but would you enjoy it for a month or two?

#2. Have you thought about living on a Louisiana bayou?

I'm sure you haven't, but that's the purpose of this section—to get you to thinking about retirement ideas that you have never thought of before. You could sit outside, watch the boats go by, talk to the locals, fish, read, write a book or just relax. You could take this concept and do it in dozens of other settings. In other words, live somewhere different, unique, and interesting for a while. If you were going to live there permanently, you would probably want a little nicer house, but could you see yourself living somewhere like this for a month or two every year? You might find yourself looking forward to the time you would spend there every year. Are you starting to see the appeal of this concept?

#3. Do you want to live on a boat?

Unless you already have the experience and skills required, you probably don't want to set out and sail around the Caribbean, but you can live on a boat in a marina or on a river, cruise the Intracoastal Waterways or live on a lake and do it without experience. Living on a houseboat requires no previous experience. There would be some things you would have to learn, but that would be part of the adventure. Of course, if you want to put the time and money into gaining the skills required, you could learn to do what is called blue-water sailing. My son lived on a boat for years. He has lived on a houseboat and a sailboat. I have friends who are sailing across the

Pacific right now. A couple of years ago, they didn't know anything about sailing. Where there's a will, there's a way. By the way, if you think you might like to live on a boat, I have written a book called *Living on a Boat—An Inexpensive Lifestyle with the Right Mix of Fun, Adventure, and Relaxation.* You can find it on Amazon at this link:

https://www.amazon.com/dp/1947020900

#4. How about traveling around the country in an RV?

Here is a picture of me camping in the Pisgah National Forest in the North Carolina Mountains. I camped there for two weeks; the cost was $2.50 a night and the view was out of this world. The trout stream behind the motorhome was nice too. If you find this lifestyle interesting, you can find out a lot more about it in Chapter 14.

#5. Maybe you have a fantasy place in the Caribbean that you've dreamed about

I think we've all dreamed of getting away from the stress and drama of the real world and just going to an imaginary place in the Caribbean or South Pacific and living carefree. It's not totally out of the question now. I'm not talking about living in a 5-star hotel on the beach. I'm talking about living in a remote, out of the way, place where you are truly away from it all. There are places where you can do this very inexpensively.

#6. Do you want to live in a different country?

Living in a different country can be relaxing, inexpensive, and enjoyable. Above is a picture of where I lived in Costa Rica for six months. It's on the side of a mountain with a wonderful view surrounded by coffee farms and banana trees. The cost was only $500 a month, and that covered everything—electricity, Wi-Fi, telephone, etc. As you might imagine, I will be going back there for a couple of months this spring. If you want to find out more about this place, you can check out the following website: www.Escape-in-Costa-Rica.com or this YouTube video I shot a few years ago:

YouTube.com/watch?v=fnp7TglpdS4

#7. Do you want to take your present house with you and move it to someplace warmer?

Maybe you're not interested in living in some exotic or remote place. But you would just like to have your present house and yard in a warmer place in the winter and maybe a cooler place in the summer. Maybe you like your house, but with the kids gone it's just too big. In Chapter 11, I will be talking about living in two different places. A lot of people find that they're happy living in two smaller houses in two different places. That's what my parents did for 20 years. They had a house in Florida and a house in Tennessee. They loved that arrangement.

#8. How about a tiny house or cabin in the mountains?

Living in a cabin in the mountains (maybe by a river or mountain stream) might be nice. I looked at a log cabin on a lake in the mountains one time. It even had a boat dock, and a canoe was included. The rent was $500 a month. It was about 35 minutes outside of Asheville, NC. I ended up not renting it, but I sometimes wish I had. It would have been a great place to get some writing done. The place even had a strong cell phone signal.

Why would a somewhat reasonable person decide to retire to any of these weird and crazy places?

After you decide to embark on one of these adventurers (or a different one that you come up with), I'm sure some of your friends will be asking (or at least wondering) why an otherwise-reasonable person would do such a weird and crazy thing.

Maybe a simple answer should be, "Why not?" Another answer might be, "I don't want to keep living the same way I'm living now or urinating away my savings in some high-priced retirement community for the rest of my life."

Have you started dreaming yet?

One thing that makes your dreaming process easier is that you're not trying to decide on a place or way to live for the rest of your life—maybe not even for a year. Later in the book, I'm going to show you how you can live in different places and have the freedom to change your mind and live somewhere else whenever you want to. That's true freedom.

You probably haven't considered any of these ideas as ways to live your retirement. I just wanted to open your mind to some new retirement ideas to consider.

Now it's time for you to start dreaming about your retirement. Get busy dreaming and keep reading.

Bottom line: Having your dream is the most important thing when it comes to planning a happy retirement. Do you have that dream?

As the words in the song from *South Pacific* say, **"If you don't have a dream, how you gonna have a dream come true?"**

Chapter 2

Can I Afford to Retire?

"Now is no time to think of what you do not have. Think of what you can do with what there is."

~ Ernest Hemingway

Yes, as old Ernest so clearly stated, now is not the time to worry about what you don't have.

Back when you were in your 20s, 30s or 40s, you could have worked out a plan for how much money you would have to save every month to have a certain amount of money when you reached retirement age, but that time has come and gone.

Now you need to look at things from the opposite end and not try to decide how much you will need to retire. What you have is what you have.

The question is, what kind of retirement life can you have with the money and income you have? It's that simple.

How much income will you have coming in?

First, look at all of the sources of money you'll have coming in—Social Security, any pensions, income from rental property, etc. What is the total? That's a good number to start with.

Two ways to retire and be financially independent

Most financial advisors will tell you how many millions of dollars you will need to retire and be financially independent. If that option is not in your immediate future, here are two easier ways to be financially independent.

#1. Spend less than you make.

#2. Make more than you spend.

Doing either one of these things will make you financially independent.

I know you want me to get back to being serious. But what I just said is deadly serious. Most people never stop to realize this fact. You can have everything you want if you will just stop wanting so many things—especially things you don't need.

Most people can do this just on their Social Security income. The average Social Security income for an individual in 2018 is $1,404. The average for a couple is $2,340.

You can live wild, free, and happy with this income.

When you get to Chapter 17, you will see several ways that retirees are stretching their money.

If you have additional sources of income, that's even better.

Add a side hustle such as being a part-time Uber or Lyft driver or any one of hundreds of other income-producing options that are discussed in Chapter 16, and you could live comfortably. Even if you're not old enough to receive Social Security yet, in later chapters, I'll show you how you can earn way more than it would take to live the lifestyles I've described.

What gets a little more complex is determining the value of any real estate, your business or other assets you have. All of these could be liquidated and turned into a monthly income, but, for now, let's see what you can do with just the cash you have coming in each month.

The good news

The good news is that you can live a wild, free, and happy retirement regardless of how much (or how little) money you have. I'm going to show you how to do it.

We've all heard (and probably said) that "money can't buy happiness." I don't think most people really believe that.

If money could buy happiness, why can't I sell some of my happiness? I have lots of happiness. I could sell some of my happiness and still be plenty happy. Some rich person who is not happy could give me some of their money, and they would still have plenty.

If I listed on Craigslist or eBay that I had some happiness for sale, do you think I would get any buyers?

I'm being facetious. Being able to afford retirement is a serious matter, so let's get back to reality.

First, let me give you an example of money not buying happiness. Last year, I was at an RV campground. There was a little old couple (in their 80s) camped there. They had been RVing full time for six months in a small pop-up camper they bought for $3,000. They were the happiest people in the campground.

There were people there living in motorhomes that I'm sure cost them well over $300,000, but they were not nearly as happy as the couple in the pop-up camper.

Go back and look at the retirement ideas I talked about in Chapter 1 when we were talking about dreams and pick out any one of them (or another one that you came up with).

It may not be immediately obvious, but it's possible to live any one of these dream retirement lifestyles for far less than you're spending living the way you're living now.

You can make more money than you spend while retired

I have some friends who went to Hawaii a few years ago and stayed for two weeks at a bed and breakfast. The couple who owned and ran the B&B said they liked their lifestyle, but they didn't like having to be there 365 days a year and never getting a break.

To make a long story short, for the last several years, my friends have been going to Hawaii and running the B&B for a month each year. They get to stay in the B&B, and they get a modest salary.

Keep in mind that you need some physical exercise when you retire. What you don't need is stress.

You're not worrying about getting the corner office, getting a promotion or a raise, and you're not taking any work home with you. Why go to the gym when you can do a little physical work in exchange for staying in some beautiful place for free (and maybe even get a small salary)?

Chapter 16 goes into great detail about the ways retirees are making money to support their retirement lifestyle, and in many cases how they are doing it without dipping into their savings at all.

Bottom line: It's true that the retirement lifestyle is not all rainbows, sunsets, and margaritas, but enough of it is that, after being retired for several years and living a variety of different fun, exciting, and low-cost lifestyles, I wouldn't want to go back to living in a conventional stick-and-brick house, condo or apartment. No way. (And I don't even like margaritas.)

Chapter 3

Money Is Not Holding You Back, It's Fear

"It's nice to get out of the rat race, but you have to learn to get along with less cheese."

~ Gene Perret

When you start thinking about retiring and living a different kind of life, one of the first things you'll start to think about is the money. In Chapter 1, I talked about a lot of unusual places to retire, and, in the process, you probably thought of even more. Some of them could get expensive and cost more than you could afford.

They could all get expensive if you let them get out of hand. How much it costs to live these lifestyles depends on how big of a boat or RV you buy, where you live when you travel to a different country, etc. Every option we talked about could be very inexpensive or extremely expensive. So, yes, money could be a problem.

But looking on the bright side, each one of the adventures previously described could be lived in a very inexpensive manner and, for sure, for a lot less than your present lifestyle is costing you.

So, face the facts, money is not really the issue. It's fear that's keeping you from acting.

Maybe you could call it reservations or concerns. Those words mean about the same thing as fear, but they sound better. No one wants to say they're afraid of making a simple lifestyle change, but it's okay to have reservations.

Here are some of the fears (I mean reservations) you might experience when you think about changing your lifestyle.

- Fear that your friends will think you're being totally irresponsible

- Fear that you'll run out of money

- Fear that you'll blow what money you have and have to come home and try to find a job and a place to live

- Fear that you won't like the lifestyle and then have to admit that you were wrong

- Fear of embarrassment when things don't work out

- Fear of not being safe

"You probably wouldn't worry about what people think of you if you could know how seldom they do."

~ Olin Miller

In other words, stop worrying about what people think about you because, contrary to what you think, most people don't think about you at all.

If you have a dream of living a different retirement lifestyle and you're not doing it yet, my guess is that fear is holding you back. It's not the money (maybe it's the fear of running out of money).

The idea of taking a risk conjures up feelings of fear. It's a normal and natural reaction. Fear helps keep us safe, but sometimes it's easy to let fear have more control over our actions than is warranted.

There's the fear of getting hurt like why we didn't want to jump off the high diving board when we were kids. That's not the fear you're dealing with here. You don't really think you might get hurt if you start living a different retirement lifestyle.

My guess is that your biggest fear is that it won't work out, and then you'll have to listen to your family and friends saying, "I told you so." Even if they don't say it, you know they will be thinking it.

Most people don't want to admit it, but these are the fears that keep a lot of people from taking the plunge and living a different retirement lifestyle.

Keep reading, and I'll show you how you can be convinced that you really can make it work and how you can live your new retirement lifestyle on a dime and a dream.

Something to think about

There's an old saying meant to remind you that you don't have to get involved with another's drama.

The saying is, *"It's not my circus and not my monkeys."* Sometimes it's good to keep that saying in mind.

But what if you look at your life and realize that this is your circus and those are your monkeys?

In other words, this is your life, and it's going to continue just as it is unless you make some changes.

Making a change involves taking a risk

A lot of people land a decent job and ride it until it's time to retire. Then they retire and continue to live in the same place and do the same thing they've done for years—which is basically nothing.

That's the safe way to live life, but you know what they say about the best-laid plans of mice and men. Things don't always work out the way you planned.

How many people do you know who thought their job was secure until they went to work one day and found out that it wasn't? It's something to think about. In other words, how much security do you have now?

If you get your living expenses low and have two or more streams of income (I'll describe how to do that later), you'll have real security. Money fears will no longer exist.

Whether you're 27, 72, or somewhere in between, you can start now and live a totally different life

Up until the last few years, retiring before you were old enough to collect Social Security was not a realistic option for most people, but now technology (and a lot of other things) has changed all of that.

It's no longer a matter of whether you can afford to quit your job and live your retirement dream. The only question is, "Do you really want to?"

Later in this book, I'll convince you that you can afford to do it, but, for now, take my word for it.

Adventurous retirement living can be inexpensive because if you stop buying so much stuff that you don't need, you'll only have to pay for housing, food, insurance, a few personal items, and that's it. That's the bare minimum, but you'll probably want to spend a little more.

I'll get into all of that later in the book.

Employers now recognize retirees as being hard-working, dependable employees. They're eager to hire them to work part time.

Lots of other income-producing opportunities for retirees will be described later in the book.

The risk of change

I have lived full time in my motorhome for six years now. Before that, I lived in Costa Rica for six months.

There are so many interesting lifestyles out there to choose from. You don't have to stick with just one—I didn't. I've already made arrangements to go back to Costa Rica to live for a few months in the spring of 2019. (Not in my motorhome, of course.)

Most people think they're locked into the way they're living now.

Society and advertising have brainwashed most of us into believing that we need to keep working, accumulating more and more stuff, taking a two-week vacation every year (when we can afford it), and be happy with that situation.

Most people have a reasonably new car or two (with payments), and they think they've achieved the American Dream.

I think you've about decided that there must be more to life than this and that's why you're reading this book.

You want to know if you have options, and, if so, how you can turn them into reality.

As you read this book, you will see that there's a whole new world waiting for you out there. You'll learn what it's like to live a wild, free, and happy retirement. You'll also learn how you can afford to live this lifestyle while putting more money in savings every year than you're doing now.

One final thought: You can't plan everything regardless of how much time you take getting everything ready for your retirement adventure. When I was in engineering school, almost all my time was spent learning how to design things. But when I started working as an engineer, I found out that I spent a lot more time testing designs than I ever spent doing the actual designs. I found out that that's the way engineering works. In school, I don't remember ever testing anything.

You've planned everything. Your testing will start when you hit the road.

You can't plan for everything. Well, you can. It's called an emergency fund.

There may be valid reasons why you can't retire right now (aging parents you need to take care of, a business or house you need to sell, etc.), but don't let fear be one of the reasons you don't retire. Fear is useful to help you make sure you've looked at all the factors involved, but it shouldn't be a reason not to take the plunge.

Retirement life can now be anything you want it to be. You can live where you want, stay as long as you want to, and move when you want. You'll have more freedom than you've ever had in your life, and you will even have the freedom to stop living one retirement lifestyle and live a different lifestyle any time you want to. What a wonderful way to live—at least that's the way I see it.

Bottom line: Don't be afraid that something will go wrong. Accept the fact that for sure something will go wrong, and then something else will go wrong. That's the retirement lifestyle. If you can't handle that, this life is not for you.

Fear will never go away completely, but as you gain confidence in your ability to handle the different situations that retirement living throws at you, fear will lose its control over you.

Chapter 4

Retire Early and Often

"Only fools and dead men don't change their minds. Fools won't. Dead men can't."

~ John H. Patterson

John Patterson started the National Cash Register Company, that became NCR. AT&T later bought it. I worked for NCR for 10 years designing computers for the banking industry.

John hired, trained, and fired a lot of people in his day. At one time it was estimated by some business historians that one-sixth of all the executives in the United States had at one time worked for John Patterson.

He would fire someone at the drop of a hat and for very little reason. He fired one manager for the way he rode a horse. He said, "If you can't manage a horse, I don't want you managing my men."

He even fired Tomas Watson, Sr. who went on to become the general manager, and then president, of CTR, which was later renamed IBM.

When I was working for NCR, we had a common joke among us engineers; we would say, "Well, if I get fired, I can always go form another IBM."

I'm pointing all of this out to say that jobs are not secure. How many people do you know of who thought they had a secure job until one day they didn't?

Maybe you should fire yourself before your boss does.

When should you retire? There's never a perfect time, but when the kids move out and the cat gets run over is a good time.

(One of my proofreaders told me that cat owners don't like jokes about dead cats and that I should take this sentence out. I guess I should, but now that I'm retired, I don't have to follow all the rules.)

Another good time to retire is when you hate going to work every morning (or even every other morning).

Money managing guru Suze Orman recently said that you should not retire a minute before you reach 70.

That might be good advice if your goal is to maximize the amount of money you will have when you retire. But if your goal is to get the most enjoyment out of your life and retire wild, free, and happy, toss Suze Orman's advice out the window in a heartbeat.

By all means, the best time to start thinking about your retirement is before your boss starts thinking about you retiring.

Let's get on with the title of this chapter and consider the option to. . .

Retire early and often

I'm sure you've heard the old joke advising people to, "Vote early and often." That wouldn't be legal, but it would be legal to retire early and often.

If you're considering retiring early and often, there are two ways to do it. One is just to retire early. You don't have to wait until you're 65 (or some magical number). I'll talk about that later in this chapter, but first. . .

How about taking a sabbatical?

The other way is to retire often by taking mini-retirements. By this I mean retire for a year or so every five to seven years.

If you did this, some people might think you were being irresponsible. Instead of saying you were going to take off from work for a year, it might sound better to say that you were going to go on a sabbatical for a year.

A lot of universities give their professors a year off with pay every seven years so that they can go on a sabbatical. Your employer probably won't give you a year off with pay, but I know a lot of people who were able to negotiate a year off without pay. You just have to ask.

Taking a sabbatical is not a new concept. It's in the Bible. In Leviticus, Chapter 25, verses 1 through 4, God told Moses to speak to the Israelites and tell them not to work the land every seventh year.

I've heard people say they would be afraid they couldn't get their old job back if they took off for a year. That's good news. You shouldn't want your old job back.

Forbes, Fortune, Harvard Review, and several major business magazines have said that you should change jobs and maybe even careers every four or five years.

Take a sabbatical, clear your mind, and start a new job or career.

After all, one definition of a career is that it's a job you've had too long.

Dream, plan, and then make it happen

When I talk about sabbaticals, most people say things like, "That would be nice, but there's no way I could ever do that."

To take a sabbatical, you have to start by dreaming about what you want to do with your year off. You can't just say you're going to be lazy and not work for a year. You could, but the new would wear off that in a hurry, and you would get bored.

You have to have a burning desire to do something exciting and special. Go back and look at the ideas suggested in Chapter 1 about dreaming. Maybe you want to get an RV and travel across the country. Maybe you want to live in a foreign country for a year. Maybe you want to live on a boat for a year.

Let your imagination run wild. Remember your goal is to be wild, free, and happy—even on a sabbatical.

Then, the next thing you have to do is plan. You don't want to blow all of your savings, so you will probably

need to cut some expenses and save some money for a
year or so. Decide what to do with your house (sell it,
rent it out, etc.). The planning phase could be an
enjoyable part of the process.

Instead of the traditional method of working and saving
until you're 65 or so and then retiring, a lot of people
now are doing this sabbatical thing. They're retiring for a
year every five years or some variation of this technique.

Their thinking is that they don't know if they will still have
their health when they reach the conventional retirement
age. And even if they do, there are a lot of things they can
do at 35, 45, or 55 that they can't do at 65 or 75.

It's a concept that most people have never considered,
but I meet people all the time who are retiring early and
often.

How many couples do you know who had great plans for
their retirement? But then, one of them died or became
too sick or disabled to live the retirement life they had
planned and worked for all their lives?

Involuntary retirement

Half of all workers are forced into retirement before
they're ready. It's called involuntary retirement. You can
have your retirement all planned out, but research data
shows that almost 50% of people retire involuntarily

before their planned retirement date because of health reasons, disability, company downsizing or to care for a family member.

Instead of letting circumstances dictate when you retire, you may want to think about retiring on your terms and doing it when you decide to do so.

Keep in mind that most of the people who died yesterday had plans for today.

One other thing to keep in mind is that, regardless of how wealthy you become, the size of your funeral will mainly depend on the weather.

"My father taught me to work, but not to love it. I never did like to work, and I don't deny it. I'd rather read, tell stories, crack jokes, talk, laugh—anything but work."

~ Abraham Lincoln

Another version of the mini-retirement

For about 20 years I traveled all over the US 11 months out of the year. I was flying to a different part of the country every week putting on seminars. I accumulated over two million Frequent Flyer miles with Delta, and I still haven't used all of those miles.

During December, I found that it was hard to get people to attend the seminars because they had Christmas on their minds.

So, since I could fly anywhere in the world free using my Frequent Flyer miles, during December every year, I didn't do any work. I just did international travel.

I camped out in Africa and hiked through the jungle to see silverback gorillas. I went to India and rode elephants through the jungle to see the tigers. I hiked through China. I went to Australia, New Zealand, Europe, South America. You name it, and I have probably been there—except I didn't go to big cities or where most tourists go.

I'm glad I did those things back then. I did a lot of the strenuous things I couldn't do now. I did run a marathon after I turned 60, and I ran a 5K race six weeks after having a heart valve replaced.

I had a heart valve replaced with a pig valve. As much bacon and barbecue as I've eaten, I'm sure it wasn't easy finding a pig that would give me a valve.

Anyway, instead of taking a year off every five to seven years, I took a month off every year.

Consider retiring early

If you don't want to try the mini-retirement method, maybe you should consider retiring at 45 or 55. Look at your situation and at least consider it.

A lot of people take a one-year sabbatical and then find a way to make it work and never go back to their previous conventional lifestyle.

If you're like most people, you continue to get promotions and raises. Then you buy a bigger house and more expensive cars. Maybe a little more goes into savings, but probably not much more.

In other words, your cost of living keeps going up to equal (or maybe even exceed) your income. All of this gives you what is considered to be a better lifestyle, but is it making you happy? A lot may depend on how much you enjoy your work. Do you look forward to going to work every day? Some people do, but a lot (and I do mean a lot) of people hate going to work every day.

What about you? Can you say that you feel wild, free, and happy? If not, you always have the option to change things.

When you retire, you may not totally stop working, but you could do something with no stress, works with your schedule, and allows you to enjoy the time you spend working.

I have a friend who was an attorney, and he quit working as an attorney 12 years ago. He and his wife live full time in an RV. He does some writing, puts on some seminars, and does some speaking. Sometimes he and his wife will work for a season as camp hosts. They will check campers in, mow grass, clean bathrooms, but they don't attend any meetings, and there's no stress.

He doesn't make as much money as he did as an attorney, but his cost of living is way less. The most important thing is that he is living wild, free, and happy.

The key to retiring early

The key to retiring early is to decide what lifestyle you would like to live (of course, you can change your mind at any time). Then find a way to cut your living expenses down to a level that will allow you to live that lifestyle.

When you venture out on your new lifestyle, you'll find that there's no longer any desire to keep up with the Joneses, drive a new car or continue buying "stuff".

Also, in your new life, you'll probably continue to do some work, but it's a different kind of work. There's no stress. You won't be worrying about getting the promotion or the corner office.

You may do some mundane type of work. You need exercise, but why spend time and money going to the gym? You can rake leaves, work in an office taking reservations, clean bathrooms, mow grass or water flowers. Look at it as exercise.

In most resort areas where you might want to live, there are plenty of jobs of this type. You might work for a free cabin or a free place to park your motorhome.

You may not be making much more than the equivalent of minimum wage, but there's no stress. You can walk away at any time. And you know it's only for a short time. It's not a job—it's exercise.

Imagine having total freedom. You can live where you want to, do what you want to, pursue your hobbies or learn a new skill.

You will have time to write a book, develop an online business, paint, learn to play a musical instrument, learn a foreign language.

Amazon recently said that they had 1,000 authors who were earning royalties of over $100,000 a year. Add your name to the list and make it 1,001.

A friend of mine is one of those 1,000 authors. He makes about $200,000 a year from the royalties on his books, and he had never written a book before in his life until just recently. He wouldn't have been able to write those books if he was still working a full-time job.

The most important thing you need to do is to make your decision and change your attitude about what's important in your life. For most people keeping their present job (as long as they can) and continuing to do what they have always done is probably the best course of action.

They had rather settle for their mundane life. The stress of making a change or taking a risk would be too much for them.

Bottom line: You know that things don't make you happy. You've already tried that. Experiences make you happy. My guess is that, since you're reading this book, you're not like most people, and you're seriously considering making a change in your life. You want to get out of the rat race. In other words, you want to retire and put some fun and adventure into your life. You want to know how to make it happen. Keep reading, and you'll soon find out.

Chapter 5

Your House Is a Burden
(Even If It's Paid For)

"Hard work pays off in the future. Laziness pays off now."

~ Stephen Wright

When you start thinking about retiring, one of the first things you have to think about is what to do with your house. This can be one of the biggest obstacles to enjoying a different retirement lifestyle.

It's easier to do nothing. Just quit work, get your gold watch (yeah, who gets one of those nowadays), and sit there in your house and do nothing. No wonder a lot of people decide that retirement is not what it's cracked up to be.

Of course, before you can do anything with your house, you have to get rid of all of the useless stuff you've accumulated over the last umpteen years. You don't have to worry about that now because what to do with all of your stuff is covered in the next two chapters. Consider that problem solved for now and let's get back to what to do about your house.

Face the fact that your house is putting a big damper on anything you think about doing.

You might think that if your house is paid for, it doesn't cost you anything to let it sit there while you're gone, but it does. It costs you either the lost monthly rent or the return on the money if you sold it and invested the money in the market or some other investment.

Any way you look at it, your house is a burden

If you're leasing a house or condo, you don't have a problem; you can walk away, but let's assume that it's not that simple. You own the house (whether it's paid for or not).

You have three options

1. You can walk out, lock it up, and hope it's okay when you come back.

2. You can rent it out for a year and then decide later what to do with it.

3. You can sell it.

Option #1 might work if you are only going to be gone for three to six months. My parents did that for 20 years. They had a house in Tennessee and one in Florida. They spent about six months in each house. Both houses were fully furnished right down to toothbrushes. When they moved to the other house every year, they didn't even pack a suitcase.

Option #2 is what a lot of people do if they're going to be gone for a year or more. It's a good option if you're not sure if you want to give up your house or not. I mostly think it's a way of kicking the can down the road. It's a way of not deciding. Some people find that the two-step process (rent the house for a year and then sell it) is the best choice. After a year of being gone from the house, you're not as emotionally attached to it, and it's easier to decide to sell it.

Option #3 is the one I would recommend if you're serious about wanting to change your life and live a different

lifestyle in your retirement. You may not know how you
want to live your retirement years right now, and, as I
will share with you in Chapter 10, it's okay to have shaky
plans. You can live one lifestyle for a while and then live
a different lifestyle.

In almost all cases, none of the ways you will want to live
during your retirement will involve you living in your
present house. You're ready for a change.

Bite the bullet and sell your house

I could have just skipped all the rambling on the previous
pages and just told you to sell your house, but I wanted
you to feel like you considered all the options and came
up with the decision yourself.

And, to be realistic, there are some situations where selling
your house is not the best decision, so you do need to
consider your situation. Just remember, the facts are not
going to change, so consider the facts and act. There's no
need to procrastinate.

Now is a good time to be selling a house and you can get
top dollar for it in today's market. Think about it, if you
wanted to stay in your house and keep doing what you're
doing now, you wouldn't be reading this book.

Finish reading this book, make your decision, carve it in Jell-O (I'll explain that in Chapter 10), and then act. Start making things happen.

You'll feel a huge relief when your house is sold

Having your house sold and the money in the bank (and your mortgage paid off if you had one) is a great feeling. It opens up so many options.

Chapter 6

Stuff Is the Killer of Joy

"Don't let the noise of others' opinions drown out your own inner voice. And most important, have the courage to follow your heart and intuition."

~ Steve Jobs

The biggest hindrance to enjoying retirement for most people is all the stuff they have accumulated.

We are all packrats by nature. We don't like to throw anything away. I think men tend to hold on to things because they think they might need them sometime. I think women hold on to things a lot of times for sentimental reasons.

Of course, that's a broad generalization and men and women both hold on to things for a lot of reasons—and sometimes for no reason at all.

I can't count the number of times I've had people tell me that they could never live a different life or live in a different place because they have too much stuff.

They never say, "I choose to have too much stuff." They act like they were born that way and there is nothing they can do about it. They never look at the situation as a choice they made or the fact that the situation could ever be changed. It's just a fact of life—at least that's the way they see it.

Getting rid of stuff is not the hard part

The hard part is deciding to get rid of stuff. It's easy after you decide you're going to do it and you want to do it.

In the next chapter, I will show you the easy way to get rid of all your excess stuff and be happy about it.

All your stuff that you need to get rid of will fall into one of two categories: It's either something you might need one day, or it's sentimental.

What about the stuff you might need?

There is always the possibility that a thing might be needed or come in handy some time. I remember buying a set of cables to connect a DVD player to a TV. I bought them at a yard sale for a quarter.

A year or so later, my mother needed a set of the cables. No problem. I had a set somewhere in storage. I spent over two hours hunting for the cables. I finally gave up and went to Radio Shack and paid $8.00 for a set of the cables. Two years later, when I was moving things out of my storage unit, I found the cables.

If I had never bought the cables, I would have immediately known that I didn't have any cables and I could have saved the two hours I spent looking for them.

When you get rid of most of your stuff, you will know what you have and where it is. It's a lot less stressful to say, "I don't have one of those," than to say, "I've got one somewhere, but I don't know where it is." It's a great feeling knowing everything you have and knowing where it is.

There is always a chance that a thing will come in handy one of these days, but it's not likely. Seven years ago, I got rid of most of my stuff and moved into a 34-ft. Class A motorhome. I knew when I got rid of all of the stuff I had accumulated that I would need some of the things sooner or later, but I decided to accept the fact and not worry about it.

The truth is that in seven years, I have never needed a single thing that I got rid of. The day may come when I will say, "I wish I had kept that," but so far, it's never happened.

What about sentimental things?

What to do with sentimental things is a big problem for a lot of people. A lot of people tell me that if they could deal with the mountain of sentimental things, they could part with the other things.

The good news is there's an easy way to handle sentimental things that will leave you happy with the outcome. Everyone who has used the techniques I will explain has been relieved and happy with the process and the outcome.

In the next chapter, I will explain in detail how to deal with all of your sentimental things. You'll be amazed at how wonderfully well the technique works, but let's not get bogged down. You first have to decide that you want to part with your stuff. There's no point trying to figure out how to do it until you've decided that you want to do it.

The joy of having all of your junk gone

I talk to people all the time who have downsized from a 2,000 square foot house to a 200 square foot tiny house, boat, RV or cabin, and, believe it or not, they all say they don't miss a single thing they got rid of.

They say it's such a blessing to have all that stuff gone. They all had trouble letting go and getting rid of useful and sentimental things, but now that the items are gone, it's such a relief. With all their useless stuff gone, they are free.

Until you get rid of your stuff, you can't imagine the joy of having it all gone. Letting go of all the junk you've accumulated over the years gives you so much freedom.

Bottom line: Whether it's something that has sentimental value or something you think you might need someday, when it's gone, you will feel joy and freedom that's hard to imagine. Don't let stuff own you and control your life. Declare your freedom from stuff and feel the joy. The next chapter will show you how to make it happen.

Chapter 7

How to Get Rid of Your Stuff

"A house is just a place to keep your stuff while you go out and get more stuff."

~ George Carlin

When people are getting ready to retire and start a new life and a new adventure, there's one problem everyone faces—what to do with all the somewhat valuable junk they have accumulated.

Even if you're not going to head off on a new life and a new adventure immediately, now that you have some free time, you need to get rid of a lot of clutter in your home and your life. This is the perfect time to do it.

I hear people say things all the time such as, "I could never leave here. I have too much stuff."

They say it with the same conviction that they would say one leg was longer than the other one. They act like they were born with all the stuff, and there is nothing they can do about the situation.

When you get rid of all the useless junk (I mean valuable stuff) you have accumulated, you open up so many options for how you want to live your retirement. Even if you're still pondering the dreams described in Chapter 1, you know you want to do something different, even if you don't know what yet. If you are tied down by stuff, your options are limited.

Get rid of your junk and then, when you're free, you can decide what you want to do.

If you need even more help, I wrote a book called *Tidying Up*. In addition to showing you how to tidy up once and for all and never have to do it again, the book also shows you how to decide what to get rid of.

Tidying Up: The Magic and Secrets of Decluttering Your Home and Your Life

Since you're trying to get rid of stuff, you don't need another book around the house. As it says in the book, buy mostly eBooks from now on and there is an eBook version of this book available. The eBook version is available from Amazon for $3.99 at the link below:

Amazon.com/dp/B01J6EVSR4

Read and follow the rest of this chapter, and you probably won't need to buy the book, but if you need extra help, the book can be your plan "B".

How to get rid of your stuff

Consider the following story to help you understand the concept.

A friend of mine told me that when she decided to live a different lifestyle, she wasn't ready to get rid of all her stuff, so she stored everything in a barn on her parents' farm.

About a year later, the barn caught fire, and everything was destroyed. She said she should have been devastated, but she found herself feeling happy and didn't know why.

Then she realized the reason she was happy was that all her stuff was gone, and she didn't have to feel guilty for getting rid of any of it. (The things she really wanted she had taken with her.)

It wasn't that she wanted any of the stuff. She just didn't want to get rid of it at the time. I think that describes a lot of us.

If you say, "I choose to have all of this stuff," then you own the situation or problem. It's easier to deal with the situation when you look at it that way.

Here are the steps to getting rid of your stuff

Your stuff can all be classified into one of four categories, A, B, C, and D.

Category A: Things you are going to use and take with you.

Category B: These are the things you can sell—your dining room table and chairs, the sofa you bought two years ago or your riding lawnmower. You can sell almost everything, and it doesn't take long to do it. Selling all this stuff is a good way to bring in some extra cash.

Craigslist is a great way to sell larger items. If you price the items right and include pictures, they will usually sell within a week. If an item doesn't sell within a week, lower the price by at least a third and list it again.

Be sure to list a phone number where you can be reached most of the time. When someone is ready to buy something, if they can't get you on the phone, they will call another person selling essentially the same type of item you're offering.

I have sold a lot of items using Craigslist. The system works great. You get a fair price, and you get it sold quickly.

For smaller items that you can ship, you can use eBay. For both Craigslist and eBay, be sure to show several good quality pictures. Pictures help items sell quickly. With eBay, you can set a reserve price, or you can auction it off and take what you get. After all, usually, whatever it sells for is what it's worth, and that's what you wanted to do in the first place—sell the item for whatever it's worth.

Category C: These are the things that you put in a garage sale on a Saturday and then take what doesn't sell to Goodwill. This way, at the end of the day, everything in this category is gone.

Category D: This category is for sentimental things. A few of these things you may want to put in storage but very few. Pictures and photo albums can all be scanned and put on a thumb drive. If you don't know how to do this, there are businesses that offer this service at a very low price.

Most people think things on this list are the hardest to get rid of, but, in fact, these items can be the easiest to get rid of if you follow the procedure described below.

First, decide who you want to have each of these things when you're dead and gone. (I know you consider that to be a long way off, but think about it this way anyway.) Then give the items to them now. If they won't take the things now, you know what will happen to them as soon as you're gone. They'll give them to Goodwill, sell them in a garage sale or throw them away. If you have a few items that you want your grandchildren to have when they're grown, you can put these items in storage if you can't convince their parents to keep the items for them.

I know that it's hard to accept the fact that a lot of things you cherish will not even be considered worth keeping by other people when you're gone. That's just a fact. Don't blame your relatives. It's not their responsibility or duty to like or value the same things you like.

A lot of the things you will be giving people will be things they will love and really enjoy having. By giving them the items now, you'll get to see them enjoy the things and you'll know the items went to the people you wanted to have them.

Don't just put things in storage—at least, not more than what will fit in the smallest storage unit they make.

If you do put things in a storage unit, consider getting rid of even those things a year from now. Some people have found it easier to get rid of sentimental things in a two-step process like this, but don't let it drag out for years and still have your belongings in storage.

In other words, put those things you think you just can't part with in storage for one year. At the end of a year, decide if you want to continue your adventuresome lifestyle. If so, give everything that's in storage that you're not going to use to your relatives. If they don't want it, sell it. If it doesn't sell, give it to Goodwill or throw it away.

It will feel like a tremendous burden is lifted from your shoulders when you have gotten rid of all the stuff you don't need.

There is some wiggle room

Now that I've convinced you to get rid of most of your stuff and shown you how to do it, let me back up and tell you that you do have a little bit of wiggle room.

Many retirees get a small storage unit, and they keep a few things there that they're not ready to get rid of yet.

I know one couple who took a picture of their empty storage unit and then threw a party and invited their friends to help them celebrate the big occasion. It was a fun time.

Plan your party now to celebrate your freedom from STUFF!

One final point: Don't go through your stuff and decide what to throw away. Go through it and decide what to keep. The best way to decide what to keep is to ask yourself, *Does this bring me joy?* If you're truthful with yourself, you'll decide that most items don't really bring you any joy, so don't keep the item. It's that simple.

Bottom line: You have all this stuff because you choose to have it. Therefore, you can choose to get rid of it. You may not believe it now, but it's such a big relief when you get rid of all the stuff you've been hanging on to for years.

Chapter 8

Planning for Your Leap into Retirement

"It's tough to make predictions, especially about the future."

~ Yogi Berra

It's not as hard to plan your leap into retirement when you don't think about it as planning how you want to live the rest of your retirement years, but rather what do you want to try first?

This chapter is short because there's not much involved in planning your retirement. Do some research, think about your options, and then make your plan.

Implementing the plan is another story. That could take some time, but coming up with your plan shouldn't take long at all. Just remember that it's a tentative plan and you're free to change it at any time (and you probably will). It's a lot easier and quicker to make a tentative plan than it is to make a permanent plan.

Trying something out as a potential retirement lifestyle is not like taking a job in Kansas and moving the family across the country. If you do that, you're stuck there, at least for a while. You can stop living on a boat (or in an RV) and decide to move to Panama (or to Thailand) in a heartbeat. And if you bought your boat at a good price, you might even make a profit on it when you sell it.

Trying different lifestyles can be part of the adventure. By all means, when you're planning your leap into retirement, keep in mind that living in two (or more) different places is a very viable and reasonable option. That's what I do.

If you can, do most of your planning before you retire. You are a lot more relaxed then. Of course, your retirement might drop out of the sky when your company announces that you're being downsized.

Take that as a big blessing. If you're downsized, you'll probably get a severance package. That's even better than just quitting.

Let the fun begin

If there were no unknowns, there wouldn't be any adventure. So, embrace the idea that unexpected good things and unexpected bad things are going to happen. Enjoy the adventure.

Bottom line: Since you're thinking about retiring, you're ready for a change. Go for it. Get rid of your house and most of your junk (I mean valuable stuff) and go for it. If you decide you don't like the retirement lifestyle you started living, then you're free to try another lifestyle—living on a boat, living on a farm, living near the ocean or living in a different country. The main thing is to make a decision and go for it.

Chapter 9

Emotional Aspects of Retirement

"All emotion is involuntary when genuine."

~ Mark Twain

As Mark Twain said, we don't have any control over the emotions we feel. They are involuntary.

We do, however, have some control over how we deal with our emotions, and that's part of what this chapter is about.

The other purpose of this chapter is to help you know what emotions to expect as your retirement gets closer and some emotions to expect after you take the leap.

You have probably already made up your mind that you're ready to retire, but you still have a few nagging concerns from time to time as you think more about the process.

You may be thinking, *Will it work for me and will I be happy?* When you're making this big of a change in your life, there will be a lot of emotions to deal with.

Yes, one big factor to consider when deciding what to do when you retire is the emotional aspect.

One of the biggest emotions you'll have to deal with is the constant gnawing feeling of "What if."

You can analyze all the numbers and the financial aspects of retirement, but you can't put a number on the emotional part. This is the biggest unknown and probably the scariest part of living your new retirement lifestyle.

Here are some of the major emotional concerns

- What will my family and friends think about my planned unconventional retirement lifestyle?

- Will my family and friends think I've lost my mind? (Some may think you're crazy—others will be sure.)

- Will I be happy?

- Am I being realistic?

- Will I run out of money?

- Is this a mistake?

- Will I get lonely?

- What if I get sick?

- Can I deal with being away from family and friends?

Retirement emotions fall into one of two categories

The emotions you will have to deal with as you approach retirement will fall into one of two broad categories—emotions you will experience before you retire and emotions you will experience after you retire. You might think, *That sounds obvious enough.* But there's more to it than that. Let me explain.

Emotions you'll have to deal with before you retire

Here are some of the emotions that will hit you and you will have to deal with before you retire. They're easier to deal with if you're expecting them.

- The finality of selling your house or moving out of your condo

- Getting rid of your stuff

- Dealing with reactions and comments from family and friends

- Going over and over the numbers and deciding if you can do it

- Dealing with all the unknowns

- The constant "what if" questions in your head

Maybe keeping the following quotes in mind will help you deal with the unknowns of your retirement adventure.

"Life is either a great adventure or nothing at all."

~ Helen Keller

"Whenever you find yourself on the side of the majority, it's time to pause and reflect."

~ Mark Twain

Emotions you'll experience after you retire and start your new lifestyle

- Being away from family and friends

- Unexpected problems and expenses

- Will my money run out?

- Do I have enough money in my emergency fund?

- Did I make the right decision?

- What if my sources of income dry up?

Feelings to expect after you start your adventure

You'll be questioning yourself for a while after you start living your new retirement lifestyle. This questioning is normal. The future is unknown, but realistically it's unknown in your present lifestyle too.

Accept the fact that the emotions and doubts you feel when you first start out are normal. They will fade quickly when the excitement kicks in. How can you feel down when every day is a new adventure?

Face the fact that there will be a huge emotional challenge when you leave your home, job, family, and friends all at once. This can be a big blow. It can even be downright scary. Accept that this feeling is normal.

One important thing to keep in mind

If you're going to be living your new unconventional retirement lifestyle with someone else, it's important to make sure both parties want to live the lifestyle you've chosen.

I've seen it time and time again. One person is gung-ho, and the other person reluctantly goes along with the idea. It can work and sometimes it does.

I've even seen cases where the reluctant person ends up liking the plan more than the one who originally proposed the idea, but that's not normally the case.

Living your new retirement lifestyle won't fix all the problems in your life

If you have emotional baggage, getting out of Dodge won't make your problems go away.

You will have a lot of emotions to deal with both before and after you take off on your new adventure. Look at your emotions as a good thing. They force you to consider all the "what if" thoughts that come to mind. These need to be considered—and maybe more than once—but at some point, you have to decide that you've considered everything and are prepared to deal with events if and when they happen.

One more important point: I've talked about several emotions in this chapter, but I haven't talked about the elephant in the room—the emotion of fear.

I didn't leave fear out because it wasn't important but because it's so important that I devoted a whole chapter to it. Remember we talked about fear back in Chapter 3.

Bottom line: If there were no unknowns, there wouldn't be any adventure. So, embrace the idea that unexpected good things and unexpected bad things are going to happen. Enjoy the adventure.

Chapter 10

Carve Your Plans in Jell-O—It's Okay to Have Shaky Plans

"It is better to have loafed and lost than to never have loafed at all."

~ James Thurber

Nobody wants people to think they're wishy-washy or that they can't make up their minds.

I say the heck with what people think. At this stage in your life, you don't have to be logical, rational or meet society's expectations. After all, you do have a firm plan.

Remember that your plan is to retire wild, free, and happy.

How you accomplish that may (and should) change from time to time. There are certain lifestyles that you can't know if you will like or not until you try them.

So, there's nothing wrong with trying a lifestyle and then deciding that you don't like it or deciding that it was fun for a while but now you want to do something else. That's part of being free. You're free to change your mind.

I can still hear my grandmother saying, "Finish what you start." We've had that philosophy pounded into us all our lives, but now we don't have time left to finish everything we want to try. We need a different strategy. Besides, my grandmother is gone, so she will never know that I changed my mind a lot and didn't finish everything I started.

Start with an attitude of "I'm going to give this a try." As soon as you decide that you've had enough of something, quit and do something else. Don't waste one of your precious minutes doing something after you've decided that it's not what you want to do.

I'm retired. My plans are carved in Jell-O

Your moto should now be, "I'm retired. My plans are carved in Jell-O." Don't be ashamed of it. Be proud of the fact that you are now free enough to change your mind on a whim.

It's okay to have shaky plans

In my opinion, it's even desirable. There are so many lifestyles to experience and so many enjoyable things to do. At this stage in your life, don't worry about what other people say, and don't continue doing anything that's not bringing you joy. Follow Dr. Seuss's advice as he stated in the following quote:

"Be who you are and say what you feel, because those who mind don't matter and those who matter don't mind."

~ Dr. Seuss

Don't play it safe all the time—take some risks

You don't want to play it safe all the time. You want to take some risks and then quickly change course when you see that something is not working out the way you thought it would.

Several major companies give annual awards for the worst ideas or the biggest failures of the year. By showing employees that it's okay to fail, they encourage risk-taking.

If you try many new ideas and innovative options for things to do and ways to live, you are going to experience what some people might call failures.

Keep this quote in mind as you try different lifestyles.

"Life does not get better by chance, it gets better by change."

~ Jim Rohn

Don't look at changing your mind about something as a failure. Give yourself an award for recognizing that what you're doing is not what you want to do, and then move on.

As soon as you decide to make a change in your life, go out for a great dinner or splurge on a nice bottle of wine (or both). In some way celebrate the fact that you're closer to finding out what you want to do and how you want to live. Then, of course, make a change.

Bottom line: Be proud of the fact that your plans are carved in Jell-O and, therefore, they're shaky.

Chapter 11

Consider Living in Two Different Places

"Millions long for immortality who don't know what to do on a rainy Sunday afternoon."

~ Susan Ertz

When you're going through all the options trying to decide where you want to retire and what you want to do, it can get frustrating.

No one place is perfect

Maybe the reason you're having trouble deciding on the perfect place to retire is because "there ain't none."

Every place has its pros and cons. On top that, there's the weather. There's no place that has comfortable weather all the time.

I wrote a book a while back, *Home No Longer Has to Be a Place*. I'm thinking about changing the title to *Home No Longer Has to be One Place*. That more clearly describes what the book is about.

Also, some people like the snow and some people (me) hate it. Some people love the summer, and some hate the hot and muggy weather with all the bugs that come with it.

I like to be comfortable. I like to step outside and not have it shock my system—hot or cold. Other people love the different seasons. To each his own.

As I've said before, my parents lived in two different places for 20 years. They had a condo in Tennessee and a house in Florida. Both places were complete right down to toothbrushes. When it was time to go to the other place, they just got in the car and took off. They didn't even pack a suitcase.

Maybe that lifestyle is in my blood or DNA. That's the way I live. They loved living in two different places. They had family and friends in both places.

You can afford to live in two places

I hear people all the time say, "Living in two places would be nice, but I could never afford to do that." The simple answer is yes, you can.

First of all, when you're living in two places, you don't live like a tourist when you're in the new area. You're a temporary resident. You can do some tourist things, but you can't go out to eat all the time and visit all of the tourist attractions. If you do, you'll end up spending money like a tourist.

Keeping two houses is easy (and can be inexpensive)

When you leave one house, you can have the cable TV, the phone, and maybe the electricity put on "vacation mode" until you get back.

The best way to save money when living in two different houses is by ensuring that one (or both) of your houses is an inexpensive house.

If you're living in a $200,000 house now, you could live in two $100,000 houses in two different places.

The two houses don't have to be equal. You could live in a $150,000 house and a $50,000 house.

You probably don't need (or even want) to have as much money tied up in housing as you have now. How about two $50,000 houses or one $50,000 house and one $20,000 house?

Or even better, how about renting two different condos for only the time you will be living in the area? Be open to alternatives. Think outside the box.

Remember, you're not trying to keep up with the Joneses anymore. One (or both) of your houses could be a very inexpensive house. There are plenty of houses in Florida (away from the beach) that you can buy for way less than $20,000.

You don't have to have a 2,500 sq. ft. house. How about something the size of a hotel suite? You need a kitchen/living room area, a bedroom, and a bathroom. Add a patio, and maybe a storage area, what else would you need to be happy? Of course, you would want the place to be clean and in a safe neighborhood.

My uncle recently sold a place like this for $12,500, and it had two bedrooms and two bathrooms—plus a couple of orange trees in the yard.

Another popular option is to rent a place to live for only the months you will be in an area. This gives you a lot of freedom. The key to being able to do this (particularly if you're doing it in two places) is that you have to get rid of even more stuff.

What would you take with you if you were going on a vacation for a month? Why would you need any more than this for three to six months? Get rid of everything else.

Okay, you could get a small (very small) storage unit in each place to keep things when you moved out for the season. After a year or so, you would probably realize that you were not using any of that stuff you had in storage.

If you can afford to live in one place, you can afford to live in two.

Maybe you want to live in three places

I've been living in two general areas for the last seven years. I have lived in different places in these areas. I generally live somewhere in the North Carolina Mountains during the summer and somewhere in Florida during the winter.

Even in the summer when I'm living in the North Carolina Mountains, I move up and down the mountain to stay where the temperature is close to perfect.

Right now, I'm near Banner Elk, North Carolina just below 4,000 feet. As it starts getting cooler, I'll head back down the mountain to lower elevations and then, in November, when all of the leaves are gone and it's no longer pretty in the mountains, I'll head to Florida for the winter.

Before I started living in a motorhome, I lived in Costa Rica for three months on two different occasions. That's what I'm going to do again this year. When it's time to leave Florida, I'm going to go to Costa Rica and live there for two or three months, but not in my motorhome.

How to go about living in two or three places

Maybe, after reading this chapter, you've decided that living in two or three different places is a good idea. The next step is to decide how to go about it and make it happen.

One way to gradually move into the concept of living in two places is to let one of the places be where you're living now. That greatly simplifies the process. Then all you have to do is decide where you would like to live for the winter or the summer.

I would highly suggest that you rent a place where you want to live for a season and see how you like it. Live there at least three to six months. I don't think you can get a feel for how you like a place by only living there for two or three weeks.

If you like living there, while you're there, you can check out the area and look for a place you can buy at a bargain price. By buying at a bargain price, if you change your mind, you can sell it in a year or so and get your money back and maybe even make a small profit.

A lot of people want to get out of Dodge and live somewhere else. Some people decide they like living part of the time in the area where they're living, but they don't need a house as big and expensive as they currently have.

One thing to consider is that a condo is a lot easier to walk off and leave for a few months. Nothing is going to freeze, there's no yard work to do, and it's not likely that anyone will break in. And, of course, it could be a lot less expensive.

Bottom line: *Neale Donald Walsch said, "The adventure begins where your comfort zone ends."*

Keep this quote in mind while you make your decision about the places you want to live during your retirement years.

Chapter 12

Consider Living Part Time in Another Country

"I looked up my family tree and found out I was the sap."

~ Rodney Dangerfield

If you decide there is no place in the United States you find interesting, intriguing, and affordable, where does that leave—how about the rest of the world?

You can search Amazon and find books telling you how great it is to retire in Thailand, Mexico, Belize, Costa Rica, Panama, Guatemala, France, Italy, and the list goes on and on.

As far as the Latin American countries, Costa Rica is a little more expensive, but it's the cleanest and most modern. I've visited most of the other countries listed above, but I haven't lived there.

Between books and YouTube videos, you can quickly learn a lot about any country you're considering.

Let selecting the country you want to live in be part of the journey and excitement.

You will find a lot of customs in other countries that are different from what you're used to at home. Their customs are not necessarily better or worse, just different.

Here are a couple of customs in Costa Rica that I found interesting

When you go to a public restroom, there will be someone sitting out front. You will either tip them or there is a fee (maybe 25 cents). It is their job to keep the restroom clean, and I found public restrooms to be very clean.

Another example of something that's different is the parking in small towns. Instead of having parking meters, there is a guy on each side of the square, and he stops the traffic so that you can get into your parking space. While you're gone the guy watches your car, and then, when you come back, you tip him, and he stands out in the street and stops traffic so that you can pull out. I like the system.

You can find fun, adventurous, and inexpensive places to retire all over the world. One of the things that make all these places inexpensive is that when you're living there, if you live like the locals and don't try to keep up with the Joneses, you won't be spending a lot of money.

Housing and food are cheap, and the country itself is the entertainment

Of course, you can spend megabucks and live in expensive resorts or high-priced houses in any country, but if you live like the locals, you can live an enjoyable and inexpensive lifestyle in a lot of different countries.

Spend some time thinking about where you would like to live for a few months. You may later decide that you want to live there permanently or you may decide that it's one of the two or three places you want to live in for part of each year.

Since you will be renting a place (at least to start with), you are free to try a different place in the country you choose or try living in a different country the next year.

I love the concept of living in a different country and here is my firsthand experience. I have lived for two or three weeks in lots of places—New Zealand, Australia, Uganda, China—and shorter periods in different European countries, but the only place I lived for several months at a time was Costa Rica.

I lived there for three months twice. You can only stay there for three months, and then you must leave for 72 hours.

There are hoops you can jump through to become a resident (you're still not a citizen). When you become a resident, you can live there and not have to leave every three months.

In TV commercials, they make the beaches in Costa Rica look so beautiful. Don't go to Costa Rica for the beaches. (There are big waves if you want to do some surfing.)

I lived up on the side of a mountain at about 5,000 feet, near the little town of Garcia. The weather was perfect at about 70 to 75 degrees almost all the time.

Below is a link to a one-minute video I created and posted on YouTube showing the place where I lived for one of the three-month visits. The price was $500 a month and that included electricity and everything.

https://www.youtube.com/watch?v=fnp7TglpdS4

There are pros and cons to living in Costa Rica. I think you will find most other countries in Latin America to have similar pros and cons. I do think you will find Costa

Rica to be cleaner and have better water quality than other Latin America countries.

Pros:

- Housing is very cheap.

- Fresh fruits and vegetables are plentiful and cheap at farmers' markets.

- The people are extremely friendly.

- New, modern buses travel everywhere. They are even on most of the back roads every 30 minutes or so, and the price is low. In other words, you don't need a car.

- The temperature is almost perfect year-round.

- Food in restaurants is low cost. Two to three dollars will get you a good meal including tax and tip.

- They have US trained doctors, and the medical facilities are modern and first rate.

Cons:

- Organic fruits and vegetables are hard to find and are expensive.

- There's a rainy season from mid-summer until December. It's sunny every morning, and then it rains hard from noon until midnight.

- Most of the roads are rough.

- During the rainy season, it's hard to keep things from mildewing.

Live like a temporary resident—not a tourist

When you're living in a different country, live like you're a resident and not a tourist. After all, you are a temporary resident. Living like a resident will be less expensive, more adventurous, and more enjoyable.

Some things to keep in mind when visiting a different country

- Before you go and while you're there, learn to speak the language—at least somewhat. You don't have to, but it makes the visit there a lot more enjoyable and interesting. In most countries, you can get by speaking very little or even none of the local language. I've spent a lot of time in countries where I couldn't speak a word of their language, but you will enjoy it more when you can at least speak and understand a few important words. The more the better.

- Don't expect things to be the same as they are where you live. If they were, why would you want to go in the first place?

- When in Rome, do as the Romans do. In other words, learn and follow the customs of the country you're visiting. Your life will be so much easier and more enjoyable.

- Enjoy and experience the differences in the country you're visiting.

Bottom line: I would recommend that you seriously consider living in a foreign country for two to three months. You can't get the feel of a country by living there for just two or three weeks.

Even if you end up deciding not to live there part of each year, checking it out won't cost you anything since it will be less expensive than living in the United States. If nothing else, it will be a wonderful vacation—but remember, don't live like a tourist. Rent a house, condo or apartment and live like a resident.

━━━━━ Chapter 13 ━━━━━

Consider Living on a Boat

"If you are lucky enough to find a way of life you love, you have to find the courage to live it."

~ John Irving

One friend who retired and is living on a boat put it this way. . .

"I had rather be lost at sea than found in a cubicle."

Living on a boat can be an inexpensive lifestyle with the right mixture of fun, adventure, and relaxation.

Since you're considering options for how you want to spend your retirement years, living on a boat is one option you should consider.

There are many reasons why people choose to live on a boat. Here are some of them:

- Freedom

- Adventure

- Fun

- Inexpensive (it can be)

- Exciting

- They want a different lifestyle

Of course, there are a lot of other lifestyles that will allow you to experience these things, but probably none will bring them all together like living on a boat.

One of the first things you will notice about living on a boat is that there's a lot more camaraderie when you're living on a boat than you'll find in your present lifestyle.

It's not the right lifestyle for everyone, but it might be for you. It's worth considering. Let's dig into it a little more.

There are three broad categories of liveaboards

First of all, let me explain that there are two meanings for the term "liveaboard". It's used to describe a boat that someone lives on, and it is also used to refer to a person who lives on a boat.

In the following section, when I'm talking about the different categories of liveaboards, I'm talking about the people who are living on the boats, not the actual boats.

The most common category is the non-cruising liveaboard who mostly stays in a slip at a marina. This person will occasionally take his boat out for a day or more and even sometimes take the Intracoastal Waterways to another marina for a weekend getaway.

The second category is the cruising liveaboard who is almost always out on the open water and maybe doesn't even have a home port. This is the much less common liveaboard (but the more romantic image of a liveaboard).

To live this lifestyle, you will need a more expensive boat and a lot of expensive equipment (electronics, navigation, extra parts, tools, and backup systems for everything—bilge pumps, radios, etc.).

There is a third category of liveaboards who just want to be "floaters." They're not going anywhere. They just enjoy living on their boat at a marina. This is the least expensive way to enjoy the liveaboard lifestyle. You don't need a lot of money or boating experience to be a floater.

You will find several liveaboards in most marinas who I would call floaters. Many of them don't think of themselves as floaters because they always have plans to be a cruiser sooner or later. They never seem to have everything fixed on their boats. They're never quite ready to sail away. Many of them have not left the marina in years. They're happy living their dream of living on a boat.

Maybe there's even a fourth category. Some liveaboards move up and down the East or West Coast with the season. Even though they are cruising, they are not usually out of sight of land, and they don't need all of the expensive equipment that open water cruisers need.

Examples of people living on a boat

First, there is the option to live on a sailboat and sail around the Caribbean (or, as my friends Jason and Nikki are doing right now, sail across the Pacific). You can watch their videos and follow their adventures on their website at https://www.gonewiththewynns.net. Note that this is a .net and not a .com URL.

This is the romantic lifestyle that comes to mind when most people think about living on a boat.

Forget about that lifestyle unless you already have experience sailing a boat and have a lot of money that you want to spend on a sailboat and the equipment required to sail on what is called the "blue water." Mark that up as a fantasy. If you want to experience this lifestyle, volunteer as a crew member with an experienced person who is going on this type of trip.

Another way to live on a boat that won't require as much money or experience (but still a lot) is to live on a powerboat and travel mainly on the Intracoastal Waterways.

Chris and Cherie live half the year in their RV (a fully geeked out converted bus) and half of the year on their powerboat. When they're on their boat, they are in the process of doing what is called making the great loop. That means they are taking their boat from the Florida Keys up the East Coast of the US and then taking canals, rivers, and lakes to get over to the Mississippi and then down the Mississippi, across the Gulf of Mexico and back to the Florida Keys to complete the great loop. They expect this trip to take them a couple of years since they are only on their boat about half of the year.

You can follow their adventures and videos on their website at this link:

https://www.technomadia.com

The two liveaboard lifestyles I've described are interesting, and something you may want to dream about, but, realistically, if you're thinking about living on a boat after you retire and want to do it on a small budget, that's not how I would recommend you go about it.

There's another common and a much less expensive way to live on a boat that we haven't talked about. You can live on a houseboat on a lake. My son did this for almost 10 years.

You can spend time anchored out in a cove part of the time and at a marina part of the time.

Whether you're on a lake or out in the ocean, when you're not at a marina, you can drop your anchor and live rent-free. Of course, there are rules you have to follow, and you're not connected to water and electricity. Also, you have to go into the marina every two weeks or so to dump your tanks and take on fresh water.

After reading this chapter, if you think you want to know more about living on a boat and want to give it more consideration, below are three books I would recommend.

These books will give you a lot more information about the pros, cons, and all of the different ways you can live on a boat. They will also give you more information about how to go about making the leap to living on a boat.

The Essentials of Living Aboard a Boat by Mark Nicholas

https://www.amazon.com/dp/B0038UGFDU

Leap of Faith—Quit Your Job and Live on a Boat by Ed Robinson

https://www.amazon.com/dp/B00F3PE5W6

Living on a Boat—An Inexpensive Lifestyle with the Right Mix of Fun, Adventure, and Relaxation by Jerry Minchey (Yep, that's me.)

https://www.amazon.com/dp/B06XVPTWPF

There are other good books about living on a boat but start with these three if you want to seriously consider the liveaboard lifestyle.

Bottom line: Living on a boat is one of the many options to consider for your retirement years. You can do it either full time or part time. If the idea intrigues you, spend some time walking around a marina and talking to some of the liveaboards. They will be happy to talk to you.

Chapter 14

Consider Living and Traveling in an RV

"Any fool can criticize, condemn, and complain—and most fools do."

~ Benjamin Franklin

I have lived and traveled full time in a motorhome for seven years, so, instead of a chapter, I could write a book about the RVing lifestyle. Oh wait, I have. I have written 10 books about living in an RV. You can find them at my website, LifeRV.com, or on Amazon at the following link:

https://www.amazon.com/Jerry-
Minchey/e/B00J49VMNW

In this chapter, I will give you an overview of what it's like living full time in an RV to help you decide if it's the right lifestyle for you.

I love the RVing lifestyle, but it's not for everyone. It's probably not even the right choice for most people, but it might be just the lifestyle you will love. Or maybe you want to live the RV lifestyle for part of each year.

A lot of RVers do this. They live somewhere for the summer months and then take their RVs and head to Florida, New Mexico, Texas, southern Arizona or other southern locations for the winter. As you probably know, they are fondly called "snowbirds" by the locals where they spend the winters.

Let me tell you a little about the RVing life, and then you can decide

You can "RV on a dime and a dream" as the title of one of my recent books says. The RVing lifestyle can be one of the most enjoyable and least expensive ways to live.

You can boondock (a term that means you're camping for free—usually on government owned land). You can get your electricity from solar panels. Then all you will have to spend money on is for insurance, groceries, and a few personal items—and, of course, you will have to buy some gas if you want to go somewhere.

There are plenty of people who are living full-time in their RVs for well under $1,000 a month. I show how to do this in several of my books. There's even a Facebook Group, *RVing on $1,000 a month or less*. There are more than 4,500 members in this group. In Chapter 16, I show you how you can easily make more than $1,000 a month while living in your RV. You can live the RVing lifestyle and not dip you're your savings—even if you're not getting Social Security yet.

A few books that will help you learn about the RVing lifestyle

I go into details about how to make this happen in my book *Secrets of RVing on a Dime and a Dream—Frugal RVing on $1,000 a month or less*. You can find it on Amazon at this link:

https://www.amazon.com/dp/B07GL61DFM

Another book you might like is *Secrets of RVing on Social Security* at https://www.Amazon.com/dp/0984496866

If you want to learn more about the RVing lifestyle, spend an evening watching some YouTube videos about the RVing lifestyle and read a few eBooks about living in an RV.

There are a lot of good books about the RVing lifestyle on Amazon. Alyssa Padgett has a new book out, *A*

Beginner's Guide to Living in an RV: Everything I Wish I Knew Before Full-time RVing Across America.

You can find her book on Amazon at this link:

https://www.amazon.com/dp/B0778WS6X4

Another book I would recommend if you're thinking about buying a motorhome is *Buying a Used Motorhome – How to get the most for your money and not get burned* (Updated March 2017) by Bill Myers.

This book saved me thousands of dollars.

You can find it on Amazon at this link:

https://www.amazon.com/dp/B007OV4TBY

I don't think you need to buy more books to decide if you want to live in an RV.

But if you have decided that you want to live the RVing lifestyle, I do think you will find that investing in a few RVing books will help show you how to make it happen in a stress-free manner. These books can save you from making mistakes and maybe even save you some money.

It's not a matter of whether you can afford the RV lifestyle. It's just a matter of whether you want to live this lifestyle or not.

Of course, this is true of most of the lifestyles I've discussed in this book.

There's no right way to RV. You will find people living the RVing lifestyle in every way imaginable.

One of the best things about the RV lifestyle is that it's so flexible

You can change your plans at any fork in the road. You can go wherever whim and chance may take you. It's a stress-free, relaxing lifestyle.

When I say RVing is a relaxed, stress-free lifestyle, have you ever see an RV parked in front of a psychiatrist's office?

Most RVers who live in their RVs full-time head south for the winter months. I do for sure. It's one of the big advantages of the RV lifestyle. You can live year round where the weather is nice.

Contrary to what a lot of people think, the RV lifestyle is not expensive. In fact, it can be much less expensive than living in a regular house or condo. You can buy RVs from $3,000 to well over $300,000. My advice is, by all means, don't buy a new RV as your first one.

Start by buying a very low-cost, used RV

Most RVers have a different RV after one or two years than the one they started with. And, surprisingly, most of them go with a smaller RV when they buy their second RV.

With this point in mind, buy a very low-cost RV (motorhome or travel trailer) to start with. Then, in a year or so, when you know more about how you like to RV and what kind of RV you want, you can sell the one you have, get your money back, and maybe even make a small profit. That is if you did a good job of searching for a bargain and a good job of negotiating.

The only way you can recognize a bargain is to know the value of the type of RV you're considering. Two of the best ways to know what an RV is worth is to know what RVs like the one you're considering have sold for recently.

The more you investigate the less you will have to invest. Remember that RV prices are a lot more negotiable than car prices. I've seen RV dealers drop the price on a used RV by 1/3 or more below the asking price in the final negotiations.

Two ways to know what an RV is worth

#1. Check the sold items on eBay. Don't look at the price people are asking for their RV. Check only the price of sold RVs.

#2. Check https://www.pplmotorhomes.com/used-rvs-for-sale. This website tells you what RVs have recently sold for. The people at ppl Motorhomes sell about 4,000 motorhomes a year, and they show you what each one sold for. Most of the motorhomes they sell are on consignment, and many are not in the best condition, so you might expect to pay a little more than the prices they show to get one in good condition, but checking the prices on their website will tell you what a particular motorhome has recently sold for.

Keep in mind that you make your money on an RV when you buy it, not when you sell it. When you sell it, you're going to sell it for about what it's worth. Your goal is to buy it for less than it's worth.

A few things to consider about the RVing lifestyle

- If you like to fix things, there is always something on an RV that needs to be fixed. If you don't like to fix things, there is still always something that needs to be fixed. Get used to it.

- Living full time in an RV won't change who you are. It won't solve all your problems.

- RVing is not all rainbows, sunsets, and margaritas.

Bottom line: It's true that the RVing lifestyle is not all rainbows, sunsets, and margaritas, but enough of it is that, after living in my RV for seven years, I wouldn't want to go back to living in a stick-and-brick house, condo or apartment. No way.

Also, consider what Steve Jobs said,

"I want to put a ding in the universe."

I think you're ready to put your ding in the universe. Go for it.

Chapter 15

Solo Retirement

"The man who goes alone can start today; but he who travels with another must wait till that other is ready."

~ Henry David Thoreau

I talk to retired people all the time who tell me that if their spouse were still around, they would love to take off on one of the adventures discussed in Chapter 1.

Some of them even tell me about the plans they had to retire and do (whatever), but that's all in the past now.

It doesn't have to be. Just because your spouse (or significant other) is no longer around (for whatever reason) it's no reason for you to stop living your life.

You may not want to do the same thing the two of you had planned. It just wouldn't be the same. But there are 101 other lifestyles you can experience—and remember, as described in Chapter 10, you can change your mind at any time because your plans are carved in Jell-O.

You don't have to settle for just one way to live all the time. You can live in two or more places. That's what I do. No one place has comfortable weather all the time.

Solo retirement is not all bad—in fact, it's great

- It's less expensive for one person to travel and live.

- It's easier to plan things when you only have to please yourself.

- You get to do what you want to do.

- And the most important thing is that staying in the same place and doing the same thing (essentially, living in the past) is the worst possible option.

I'm not saying that doing what you had planned on doing with your significant other would not have been more enjoyable than living the solo retirement life, but that can't be now, so get started with plan B (which is solo retirement living).

I have been living solo in my motorhome for seven years. As I travel, I meet a lot (and I do mean a lot) of solo RVers—I think more women than men.

They are all enjoying their lifestyle and their freedom.

(Of course, I guess if they were not enjoying the lifestyle, they would be doing something else and I wouldn't meet them.)

One more thing

If you don't want to continue living your life by yourself, you have to take some steps to make something happen.

Realize that when you're out living life in one of the ways described throughout this book, you are a lot more likely to meet someone who will have your same interests and want to live and enjoy the same life you're living.

After all, if you could find someone to share your dreams by living the way you're living now, don't you think you would have already found them?

What about security?

Safety and security concerns mainly grow out of fear of the unknown. It's human nature to fear the unknown.

If there were no unknowns, there would be no adventure. How much fun would that be?

Here's what Helen Keller had to say about security:

"Security is mostly a superstition. It does not exist in nature, nor do the children of men as a whole experience it. Avoiding danger is not safer in the long run than outright exposure. Life is either a daring adventure or nothing."

~ Helen Keller

If Hellen Keller wasn't afraid, why should we ever be shaking in our boots?

When you realize that security is not a problem for you as a solo retiree, what else is there to worry about?

You could say, "What about money?" I'll cover that in the next two chapters and you will see that money is not something to worry about at all. You'll agree with me after you read the next two chapters.

Take another look at old Henry's quote at the beginning of this chapter about the fact that when you're alone, you can start when you want to. Ponder what he said.

Bottom line: Don't live in the past with thoughts of *what if* or *if only.* Grab life by the horns and live your life to the fullest. You are completely free to do it (that is if you have followed my advice in Chapters 6 and 7 about getting rid of your stuff).

So, as Mark Twain said, "Throw off the bowlines. Sail away from the safe harbor. Catch the trade winds in your sails. Explore. Dream. Discover."

================ **Chapter 16** ================

Ways Retirees are Making Extra Money

Live your life so you can say, *"When I grow up, I want to be like me."*

~ Anonymous

There are so many options now for how retirees can make money that a whole book could be written about how to do it—oh wait, a book has just been written about how to make money on the road.

It was written by William Myers, author of the popular series of adventure novels in the *Mango Bob* series. By the way, the latest book in that series is called *Mango*

Digger, and it's my favorite of all of the books in the series.

Back to making money on the road; the book I am talking about is called *Road Cash.* That's a fitting title because that's what the book is all about.

By the way, when I talk about making money while living on the road, I consider living five months in one place and seven months in another place or living in a different country as living on the road. I consider the term "living on the road" to mean not living in one place all the time.

The book came out not long ago and is up to date. It goes into great detail about more ways that are being used to make money while living on the road than you could ever imagine.

If you're even remotely thinking about wanting to make some extra money when you retire, invest $3.99 and download this eBook. You can find it on Amazon at the link below:

Amazon.com/dp/B0721832MD

A printed version of the book is available also, but I like the eBook version since it allows me to click on the links without having to type them into a browser. And, trust me, you will want to check out many of the links provided in the book.

The book describes ways to make money using your computer and ways to make money without using a computer.

The techniques described in this book are not ideas about how you might make money, but, rather, the book describes the techniques people are using to make money and support their new lifestyle.

You need multiple sources of income

I firmly believe that you need multiple sources of income if you're living on the road. Heck, my opinion is that you need more than one source of income even if you're not living on the road.

If you only have one source of income and it goes away (and it can happen in a heartbeat), you're up the creek.

I don't want to jeopardize my lifestyle by relying on just one source of income.

Some sources of income take time before the money starts coming in (such as writing a book, producing videos, etc.), and some sources start producing income immediately. I think it's good to have both types of income.

Selling items on Amazon and on eBay give you immediate income. I sell items on both sites.

How I make money on the road

Writing books and selling them on Amazon. This is by far the most profitable project I have for the time spent, and it brings in the most income. The thing I like best about this technique is that I do the work once and it continues to bring in income year after year. I use Amazon to sell the eBooks, and I use CreateSpace.com in Charleston, South Carolina (which is now owned by Amazon) to print and deliver the printed books to Amazon. If you haven't published a book before, start by writing a how-to book. They don't sell as well as novels, but they're so much easier and faster to write.

Posting videos on YouTube. I'm just getting started on this project. I like it because, as with writing books, you do the work once and get paid year after year. There's a lot to learn—not only about how to shoot and edit videos but also about how to rank high on YouTube's list of videos. The good news is there are a lot of videos on YouTube showing you how to do all of these things.

More about of making money

The most important thing is to make money by doing something you enjoy.

Keep in mind that, even if you don't have the skills required to do one of the jobs you find interesting, with all of the books and videos available, you can learn how to do almost any job in a short amount of time. You don't have to be an expert to start earning an income doing something. You just need to be a little better at it than the average person—and that's not hard to do in a lot of cases.

Making money while living on the road has never been easier. Even a few years ago, many of the techniques people use to make money now were not even possible.

Bottom line: There's no one technique that's right for everybody. Look at all of the income-producing techniques described in this chapter (including the ones described in the *Road Cash* book) and see if you don't find several that match your skills and interests and will allow you to make a lot more than you will need to support your retirement lifestyle.

Chapter 17

How Retirees are Stretching Their Money

"I was going to buy a copy of The Power of Positive Thinking, *and then I thought: What damn good would that do?"*

~ Ronnie Shakes

If you like to go shopping, buy new clothes, buy the latest gadgets, go to concerts and sporting events, like new cars, want the latest cell phone, and like to eat out all the time, you're going to end up spending as much (and maybe even more) money after you retire as you're spending now because. . .

Retiring won't change who you are

You have to make a conscious effort to change your ways. One of the first things you have to do to retire on a dime and a dream is to find ways to live and not spend so many dimes.

Stop buying stuff

One of the best ways to get your living expenses down is to stop buying stuff. Going shopping should no longer be a form of entertainment. In addition to saving a lot of money, another reason to stop buying things is that when you start living your new lifestyle, you won't have room for stuff.

Adopt the habit of getting rid of something every time you buy something new. If you buy a new pair of shoes, throw out an old pair. When you're considering buying something, ask yourself, *What am I going to throw away?* That may keep you from buying the item being considered.

I don't mean you should just cut back. I'm saying that you should stop buying stuff altogether (well almost).

How retirees save money

Your best option to save money is to make changes in areas where most of your money is being spent. You can't save any money by cutting back on how much you spend on salt because, if you totally eliminated salt, it wouldn't save enough to matter.

I know, I'm being facetious, but I'm doing it to make a point. It reminds me of the mother who said to her kid, "If I've told you once, I've told you a million times. Don't exaggerate."

I got off track. Let's get back to how retirees save money.

To save money, you have to cut back in the areas where you'll be spending a lot of money. Keep detailed records of every penny you spend for a month or so, and you might be surprised at the areas where you're spending money.

Armed with this information, you can make some informed decisions about where and how to cut back on your spending.

When you're retired, here are three areas you need to look at closely

- **Eating out:** First, don't eat out very often. Make it a special occasion. If you eat out a lot, then it's no longer a special occasion. Also, skip the chain restaurants and the tourist places. Eat at the local mom and pop places, and you will get to experience the real cuisine of the area.

- **Don't waste food:** Even if you eat most of your meals at home, you may still be wasting a lot of money by throwing away too much food. One way to save a lot on food is to start planning every meal by looking in the refrigerator and seeing what leftovers you have and then thinking what you would need to add to those leftovers to make a good meal. We're all guilty of leaving leftovers in the back of the refrigerator too long and then throwing them out. And we all know ways to save when buying food. We just don't do it. Cut out junk food, shop at discount stores like Aldi, buy mostly real food—beans, rice, veggies—and cut back on protein and high-priced cuts of meat. Also, watch fruits and veggies closely and be sure to eat them before they go bad.

- **Save money on clothes:** When you're living in a small place (which you will most likely be doing after you retire), you won't have room for a lot of clothes. You probably have enough clothes to last you a long time before you will ever need to buy more.

And when you do need more clothes, go to Goodwill or a thrift shop. There was a time when people tried to keep it a secret that they shopped at Goodwill. Now they brag about it. I was sitting around a campfire not long ago, and one woman commented to another woman that she liked her shirt. Her reply was, "I got it at Goodwill for $4."

A friend of mine's father died recently. My friend had gotten rid of all of his suits and sports coats when he retired. He went to Goodwill and paid $5 for a sports coat to wear to his father's funeral and then, on the way home from the funeral, he stopped and donated it back to Goodwill.

If you could get these three categories down to zero, your retirement lifestyle wouldn't be expensive at all. Of course, you can't get them down to zero, but, for most people, these expenses can be cut way down and without any decrease in quality of life or enjoyment—just follow the advice I've outlined.

One other point—don't be a tourist. One of the best ways retirees have found to save money is by stopping being tourists. Many new retirees spend a lot of money when they first retire because they act like they're on vacation and do things as though they are a tourist—eating out a lot, spending money on tourist attractions, and just generally acting like they're on vacation.

Remember that you're not on a full-time vacation and you're not a tourist. If you do all of the tourist things, you're going to blow your budget in a hurry. I've had several retirees tell me that they spent a lot more money the first year they were retired than they do now. They say that it's more fun to be a temporary resident in an area than it is to be a tourist, and, of course, a lot less expensive.

Save and splurge

One advantage of saving a lot of money is that it gives you more money to spend on things that make you happy. You can do a few tourist things, and buy a few gadgets, but only a few.

I don't spend much on clothes, and I don't eat out a lot. (I do like to go out and have a glass of wine and listen to live music from time to time.) Another area where I have to watch my budget is that I like gadgets, especially electronic things.

Bottom line: Follow the advice in this chapter, and you can cut your retirement expenses way down. And when you're not spending much money, you'll find that life is so much more enjoyable.

Chapter 18

Make a Decision

"Most people who died yesterday had plans for today."

~ Unknown

You've made decisions all your life, and some of them have been difficult and had a major impact on your life.

For example, what if you had to decide whether to take a job in Seattle or Dallas? Moving your family across the country to a new city would be stressful, not only for you but for everyone in your family.

And it's not a decision that you could easily reverse. If you decided that you didn't like the new job or the new city, it wouldn't be easy (and most likely not even possible) to go get your old job back and buy your previous house back.

That's not the case when you make decisions about retirement. First of all, even if you decide that you don't like the decision you made, going back to your big house is probably not what you want to do.

Also, in most cases, you're not deciding about what you want to do for the rest of your life. You're deciding about what you want to do for the next three to six months.

If you want to live on a boat or in an RV *someday*, it will never happen. I meet people all the time, and when I tell them I live full time in a motorhome, they say, "That's what I want to do one day."

They'll never do it. They're not making any serious plans to live in an RV. To them, it's just a daydream. Keep the quote at the beginning of this chapter in mind, and don't let it happen to you.

I was sitting in a marketing class at Harvard one day. The head of the marketing department was teaching the class, and the class was discussing a case.

The professor called on one guy and asked him what he would do in the situation described in the case. The student said he would go out and get more information. That was the wrong answer. Here's what the instructor said:

"Every decision you make for the rest of your life will be made with incomplete information."

He said, "Make a decision, and if it turns out to be wrong, you can change it. If you don't make a decision, the problem can never be fixed."

He went on to add, "More businesses have failed because the owners didn't make a decision than ever failed because they made the wrong decision."

I think this same advice applies to life as well.

In my opinion, it's okay to be sitting in a rocking chair on the front porch of a nursing home and saying, "I thought about living full time in an RV or living on a boat (or whatever), but after I checked into it, I decided not to do it."

I would hate to be sitting in that same rocking chair and saying, "I thought about living full time in an RV or a boat, but I never got around to deciding whether to do it or not."

Don't be like the person sitting in the rocking chair who never got around to choosing. Make a decision.

Amelia Earhart said it best: "The most difficult thing is the decision to act, the rest is merely tenacity. The fears are paper tigers. You can do anything you decide to do. You can act to change and control your life."

Almost all of your life, where you have lived has been dictated to a large extent by jobs or school or family or, let's face it, just plain habit.

Now you have freedom (because you declared that you have it), and this is your chance to make a decision with the main criteria being, *Where will I be the happiest and what lifestyle will I enjoy the most?*

If you have the dream and the burning desire to make it happen, then make a decision and go for it.

Bottom line: Do a reasonable amount of research, soul-searching, and fact-finding, and then make your decision. You will never have all of the information, but remember when you're living your new retirement lifestyle, it's easy to change your mind and live a different lifestyle.

The important things are to have a dream and to decide.

Set a Date, Then Make It Happen

"Don't wait. The time will never be just right."

~ Napoleon Hill

We are all procrastinators by nature and by habit. We've been making decisions and then putting off acting all our lives. In a lot of cases, we even put off making decisions. It's just human nature.

Some people make things happen, some people watch things happen, and some people wonder what happened. To live a wild, free, and happy retirement life, you have to be a person who makes things happen.

Look at it this way, if three birds were sitting on a fence and one decided to fly away, how many would be left? If birds are anything like us humans, there would probably still be three birds on the fence. Just because one bird decided to fly away doesn't mean he actually did it. We decide to do things all the time and then never do them.

Hopefully, you have already done the two hard things. You've made the decision, and you've set the departure date. But maybe that's not completely true.

My guess is that you've kind of made the decision about what you want to do and where you want to do it, but you haven't actually set a firm departure date.

That's your old way of thinking. Things are going to be different now. So, nail down the retirement life you want to live (you can always change your plans later), and then mark the date on your calendar.

Now you have to **make things happen**.

You can't say, "I'm going to hit the road and start my adventurous retirement life when I get everything taken care of or when (fill in the blank)." If that's your approach, it will never happen.

There are a lot of steps involved

To make your dream of living your retirement life in a wild, fun, and happy manner come true, there are a lot of things that have to be done.

Everything has to fall (or be pushed) into place to make your new lifestyle a reality.

There are so many things you have to do or make decisions about that it's hard to even know where to start. It can seem overwhelming.

Of course, one of the first things you have to decide about (and then act on) is what to do with your house.

If you're living in a rented apartment or condo, things are a lot simpler. The day your lease expires could be the day you start your new life.

Selling your house

If you own a house, things can get complicated. One of the first things you need to do is take steps to get your house sold or rented. This will be one of your biggest obstacles. Take steps to solve this problem as soon as you make your decision to retire.

Call a real estate agent and get your house on the market to sell or rent. Tell your real estate agent that you want to set a price that will make your house sell in a reasonable amount of time. Then listen to what she tells you.

Don't sit around idle and wait for the house to sell. Since you've already set a date when you're going to start your new life, get busy taking care of the other things that must be done.

A word about selling your house. I know people who have had their houses on the market for two or three years, and they still haven't sold them. A lot of people have an unrealistic expectation about what their houses are worth. Don't fall into this trap. It's worth what it will sell for now.

The main reason a house doesn't sell is that the owner has set an unrealistic price. Set your price at the fair market value (or maybe a little less), and your house will sell. Right now, houses are selling fast, so if you have set a fair price for your house, it will sell.

Put your house on the market, set a fair price, and if it doesn't sell within a reasonable amount of time, lower the price and keep doing this until it sells or until you decide to keep the house and rent it out. At that point, get it rented.

One other thing to be prepared for is that your house might sell within a few days. I was talking to a couple recently, and they said they had a contract on their house three days after they put it on the market. They had to get rid of everything and vacate the house in 30 days. My brother had a full-price contract on his house three hours after he put it on the market.

Another friend sold her house for the full asking price about two weeks after it was listed. Houses are selling fast now and usually at or near the asking price.

Normally, getting a contract on your house is a good thing, but if you're not ready for it to be sold, you might have to get ready pretty quickly.

A few years ago, my neighbour had her place on the market for over a year and then finally sold it for less than what she had turned down a month after it was listed. Your house is worth what it will sell for now.

My mother and father sold their house (and a lot of the stuff inside it) at an auction. Maybe you're not that brave, but a good auction company will get you a fair price for your house. I'm not recommending that you have an auction to sell your house, but, if all else fails, it's an option.

If you don't have a deadline, you will never get to the end of your to-do list.

Not everything has to be done before you start your adventure

You are not like Lewis and Clark heading off into the wilderness for two years. You can do things while you're on the road.

Concentrate on taking care of the things that absolutely must be taken care of before you leave. Remember, you have a departure date. If you didn't get your riding lawn mower sold, give it to somebody. You'll be surprised how fast things happen when you do have a firm departure date.

You always have the option of renting a storage unit for those items you're not ready to part with.

The next step is to start making things fall into place

After you set a date, act. As I said before, the hardest thing for most people to do is to get rid of most of their "stuff," so start this process early—like now.

Adopt Larry the Cable Guy's motto of "Git-R-Done." Another saying I like is, "Done trumps everything."

Not everything on your list will get done. Not everything has to be done before you leave.

It's more important that you get things done than it is to get them done perfectly

You've been told all your life to do your best, but not everything needs your best effort.

For example, consider the situation where you're baking cupcakes and they crumble when you take them out of the pan. If you're baking them for the Cub Scouts, just put more icing on the cupcakes and serve them.

On the other hand, if you're baking cupcakes for the bridge club, maybe you better start over and bake another batch.

My grandmother would roll over in her grave if she heard me say this, but. . .

If something only halfway needs doing, only halfway do it

That's the way it is with getting ready to live your new retirement lifestyle. Not every step in the process requires your best effort.

It's more important that you get rid of your stuff than it is to get the very best price possible for each item. Keep the big picture in mind and make sure you're making progress (and getting things done on schedule).

Once you've decided to retire from your job and live the retirement lifestyle, don't waste time second-guessing yourself.

Six months or a year down the road, you can re-evaluate the situation, and if living the lifestyle, you thought you would like to live isn't making you happy, you can change your mind and do something completely different. Remember, your plans are carved in Jell-O. You're not permanently locked into your initial decision.

People ask me how long I am going to continue living the lifestyle I'm living. My answer is simple: "Until it's no longer fun."

Back to reality

You made your decision before you got to this chapter. Don't keep rethinking your decision. This chapter gave you an overview of how to make it happen. Now it's your job to follow through, implement the steps outlined, and make it happen. Get busy.

Bottom line: As you get closer to your retirement date, it will start to feel like crunch time. There will be a ton of things that will still need to be done and not much time to do them. Don't give in to changing your departure day. If you change it once, you'll change it again and again, and the process could drag on forever.

You've handled crunch time and deadlines all your life, you can handle one more. This one is important. Make it happen. After all, you have a dream.

Chapter 20

Summing It All Up

"Grow old along with me. The best is yet to be. . ."

~ Robert Browning

Hopefully, reading this book has opened your eyes to a world of different opportunities for your retirement that you had not realized was available to you.

In other words, you now have options that you didn't know existed.

In my opinion, retirement life is a lot more fulfilling, fun, and relaxing when you choose two or more lifestyles.

Don't do the same thing all the time and don't do it in the same place.

On a personal note

I have been living in my 34-foot motorhome for the last seven years. I live in different places in the North Carolina Mountains in the summertime, and I go somewhere in Florida for four or five months in the winter. I have lived on both the Gulf Coast and the East Coast of Florida. Each area has its pros and cons.

The same is true of the North Carolina (and sometimes Tennessee and Virginia) Mountains. It's August now, and I'm up near 4,000 feet. I'll go back down the mountain to lower elevations as it starts getting cooler.

I lived in Costa Rica for six months a while back, and I will be going back there in the spring for two months when I leave Florida. Then I'll get back in my motorhome and head for the mountains again.

The way I live is only one of the many ways to enjoy retirement. When you follow the advice in this book, you can change your lifestyle at the drop of a hat. That's the beauty of the lifestyles I've described.

One of the many things I love about my lifestyle is that I'm always around people (old and young) who are making decisions and doing things. My life is never boring.

Hopefully, now that you've read this book, you have your dream clearly defined, you know what you want to do, and you know how to make it happen.

My guess is that you want to get rid of your stuff, hit the road, live in more than one place, and never look back.

If that doesn't describe you, then you probably stopped reading this book way before you got to this point.

I've shown you how to live on a dime (or at least on a lot fewer dimes than you're spending now), and I've even shown you ways to make an extra dime or two to make life on the road even more enjoyable.

And when I say, "life on the road," living in one place for four months and then somewhere else for eight months is one definition of "life on the road". You don't have to travel all the time to be wild, free, and happy.

You're ready to get started

But I want to caution you (as I said in Chapter 2); retirement is not all rainbows, sunsets, and margaritas. I get carried away sometimes when I'm talking about retirement lifestyles, and I'm sure I make them sound more glamorous than they are.

I think I've talked a lot more about the pros than I have the cons. This implies that living one or more of these retirement lifestyles would be the best choice for almost everyone.

In reality, I think just the opposite is true. When I think of all of the people I know—relatives, close friends, and general acquaintances—in almost every case, after thinking about it, I realize that most of them would not enjoy this lifestyle.

Therefore, I have concluded that the lifestyles I've described in this book are not for most people. They're only for people who love adventure and are not afraid of change or the unknowns. My guess is that this describes you.

You can live the life I've described and have everything you want

People can be happy with less because they have everything they want. Anybody who lives on less because they choose to already has everything they want. The secret is to change your wants. You no longer need to keep up with the Joneses to be happy.

I don't want to make any of the retirement lifestyles I've described sound like the perfect lifestyle. Describe things the right way and you could make almost anything sound like fun. Remember, Tom Sawyer convinced his friends that whitewashing a fence was fun.

A final thought about choosing your retirement lifestyle

Making this big a change in your life will result in an upheaval of everything you know. There will be risks, and they will result in stress. Accept this as normal, deal with the stress, and go on with your life.

As of now, adventure is in your blood. I think your decision has already been made, so set a date and make it happen. The timing will never be perfect, so make it happen now, and start enjoying your new lifestyle.

Hit the road and soak in whatever slice of nature you can. Breathe in deeply and experience the calm of the wilderness (a wilderness is anywhere that's new to you). Feel renewed and live a life with no stress. What are you waiting for?

Bottom line: Remember this:

"People don't take trips, trips take people."

~ John Steinbeck

If you're ready for a trip to take you, it's time to make it happen. Set your departure date and then hit the road.

If you have any questions for me, feel free to email me at

Jminchey@gmail.com

I would love to hear from you.

Did You Like This Book?

If you liked this book, I need your help.

I would appreciate it if you would take a minute to leave a review on Amazon. (You really can do it in only one minute.)

Writing a review is not like writing a high school book report. All you need to do is write a sentence or two saying that you liked the book.

If you would like to get in touch with me, you can reach me by email at

Jminchey@gmail.com

Thank you,

Jerry Minchey

P.S. On the following pages are some of my other books that you might find interesting and entertaining.

(You can find them on Amazon.)

Other books by the author available on Amazon

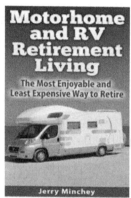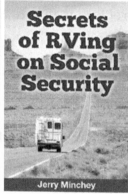

More books by the author
available on Amazon

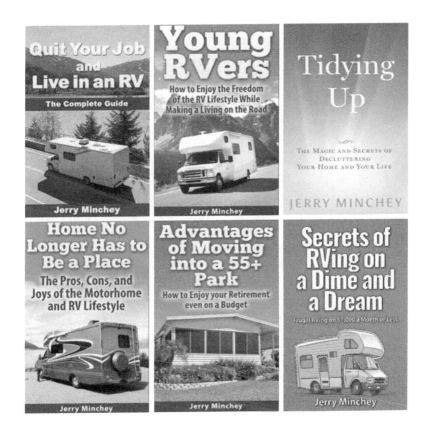

63000573R00088

Made in the USA
Columbia, SC
08 July 2019